Social Media

Connect with a community of *Bible Studies for Life* users. Post responses to questions, share teaching ideas, and link to great blog content. **Facebook.com/BibleStudiesForLife**

Get instant updates about new articles, giveaways, and more. **@BibleMeetsLife**

The App

Simple and straightforward, this elegantly designed app gives you all the content of the Small Group Member Book—plus a whole lot more—right at your fingertips. Available in the iTunes App Store and for Android devices; search "**Bible Studies for Life**."

Blog

At **BibleStudiesForLife.com/blog** you will find magazine articles and music downloads from LifeWay Worship. Plus, leaders and group members alike will benefit from the blog posts written for people in every life stage—singles, parents, boomers, and senior adults—as well as media clips, connections between our study topics, current events, and much more.

Training

For helps on how to use Bible Studies for Life, tips on how to better lead groups, or additional ideas for leading this session, visit: **www.ministrygrid.com/web/biblestudiesforlife.**

Awake: The Call to a Renewed Life
Bible Studies for Life: Small Group Member Book

© 2015 LifeWay Press®

ISBN: 9781430034964

Item: 005680985

Dewey Decimal Classification Number: 269

Subject Heading: SPIRITUAL LIFE \ RELIGIOUS AWAKENING \ REVIVALS

Eric Geiger
Vice President, Church Resources

Ronnie Floyd
General Editor

David Francis
Managing Editor

Gena Rogers
Sam O'Neal
Content Editors

Philip Nation
Director, Adult Ministry Publishing

Faith Whatley
Director, Adult Ministry

Send questions/comments to: Content Editor, *Bible Studies for Life: Adults*, One LifeWay Plaza, Nashville, TN 37234-0175; or make comments on the Web at *www.BibleStudiesforLife.com.*

Printed in the United States of America

For ordering or inquiries, visit *www.lifeway.com*; write LifeWay Small Groups; One LifeWay Plaza; Nashville, TN 37234-0152; or call toll free (800) 458-2772.

All Scripture quotations, unless otherwise indicated, are taken from the Holman Christian Standard Bible®, copyright 1999, 2000, 2002, 2003, 2009 by Holman Bible Publishers. Used by permission.

Bible Studies for Life: Adults often lists websites that may be helpful to our readers. Our staff verifies each site's usefulness and appropriateness prior to publication. However, website content changes quickly so we encourage you to approach all websites with caution. Make sure sites are still appropriate before sharing them with students, friends, and family.

D1451394

Don't sleep through your spiritual life. Wake up!

Nothing refreshes like a good night's sleep. And who doesn't enjoy the occasional afternoon nap?

In at least one way, though, sleep is not good for us. In fact, it can be dangerous. I'm talking about being spiritually asleep. Life has a way of lulling us to sleep spiritually. If we allow ourselves to settle into a spiritual snooze, after a while we simply wither spiritually.

It's time to wake up!

Our greatest need as believers—your greatest need as a follower of Christ—is to experience spiritual renewal from God. That's the whole point of this study. I must warn you, though: this is not a study for those who want to maintain the status quo. When the Holy Spirit begins to bring renewal in our lives, things *will* change.

In the following pages, we will look at several places in the Bible where God called people to return to Him. Those passages are a call for us, as well—a call to experience revival and awakening both personally and in our churches.

When people have turned back to God throughout history, He has done extraordinary things and sparked great movements. Wouldn't you like to see God do that again? Join me on the journey of asking God to bring about the next great movement of renewal and turning the nations back to Him.

Ronnie Floyd

Ronnie Floyd has served as the Senior Pastor of Cross Church in Northwest Arkansas for over 28 years. In addition to serving as the general editor for *Bible Studies for Life*, Dr. Floyd is the president of the Southern Baptist Convention. Read Ronnie's blog at *RonnieFloyd.com*. Follow him on Twitter *@RonnieFloyd*.

contents

SESSION 1

RETURN TO GOD

What's a great way to catch your attention?

#Awake

QUESTION #1

BIBLE STUDIES

God's call to return to Him demands a response.

THE BIBLE MEETS LIFE

"How did I end up here?" It's a common question. We start out with good intentions. We want to be great parents, do well in school, or take care of our health. But we falter somewhere along the way. It may be subtle at first, but after a while we look back and realize we're not the people we wanted to be. At that point we often wonder, *What does it take to get back on course?*

The same cycle can happen in our relationship with God. Laziness, a lack of priorities, and even outright sin has a way of lulling us to sleep in our daily walk with Jesus.

So here's the big question: if you get off track, what will it take to get your attention and bring you back to God?

In the Book of Jonah, we see a man who got off course in His relationship with God. Jonah's move away from God's instruction wasn't subtle; he flatly refused to listen to God. But God got Jonah's attention in a most unexpected way. As we'll see in this study, God often acts to get our attention and draw us back to Him.

WHAT DOES THE BIBLE SAY?

Jonah 1:1-3; 3:1-5,10 *(HCSB)*

1:1 The word of the LORD came to Jonah son of Amittai:

2 "Get up! Go to the great city of Nineveh and preach against it, because their wickedness has confronted Me."

3 However, Jonah got up to flee to Tarshish from the LORD's presence. He went down to Joppa and found a ship going to Tarshish. He paid the fare and went down into it to go with them to Tarshish, from the LORD's presence.

3:1 Then the word of the LORD came to Jonah a second time:

2 "Get up! Go to the great city of Nineveh and preach the message that I tell you."

3 So Jonah got up and went to Nineveh according to the LORD's command. Now Nineveh was an extremely large city, a three-day walk.

4 Jonah set out on the first day of his walk in the city and proclaimed, "In 40 days Nineveh will be demolished!"

5 The men of Nineveh believed in God. They proclaimed a fast and dressed in sackcloth—from the greatest of them to the least.

3:10 Then God saw their actions—that they had turned from their evil ways—so God relented from the disaster He had threatened to do to them. And He did not do it.

Nineveh (1:2)—Located on the east bank of the Tigris River across from the modern day city of Mosul, Iraq. This city served as the capital of the Assyrian Empire during its height.

Tarshish (1:3)—While the exact location of ancient Tarshish is uncertain, the most probable location is Spain. It was in the opposite direction from where God wanted Jonah to go.

Sackcloth (3:5)—Sackcloth is a scratchy, black-wool cloth usually made of goat hair. People in ancient cultures wore garments made of sackcloth as an expression of deep, personal distress.

Jonah 1:1-3

Jonah should have said "yes" to God. He should have obeyed. But he didn't.

God called Jonah to go to the city of Nineveh and call the people there to turn away from their sin. Nineveh had "more than 120,000 people who cannot distinguish between their right and their left" (4:11). It was a big city. It was also a pagan place, full of clueless people. God wanted to use Jonah to get their attention and do something about their spiritual condition.

How did Jonah respond? He ran in the opposite direction. It's almost comical that Jonah thought he could actually run from God's presence—almost. Jonah failed to realize he could never escape God's attention. God sees all and knows all.

When God brought a massive storm against Jonah's boat, he finally began to see the precariousness of his rebellion. Jonah knew he was under God's judgment because of his disobedience, and he was risking the lives of everyone on the boat with him (see 1:4-16). Jonah thought Tarshish would be far enough to escape God's call on his life. He found a ship to take him there, but his journey ended in disaster.

The same principles are at work in our lives. There are times when God gives us a clear call to return to Him, but we respond by taking the first ship going in the opposite direction. We race toward a place, person, or desire we think will bring fulfillment, yet we only find destruction. **Running from God always leads to pain.**

Thankfully, the story doesn't end there.

Why is it sometimes tempting to flee from God?

QUESTION #2

Jonah 3:1-5

Tossed overboard to spare the ship and its crew, Jonah was miraculously swallowed by a "huge fish" (1:17). He spent three days and nights inside that creature. It's not surprising that Jonah was moved to pray and worship God during that unprecedented interlude, and he vowed to obey God's command (see 2:1-9). When the timing was right, God caused the fish to vomit Jonah onto dry land.

Try to picture the scene: Jonah lay on the sand—exhausted, filthy, and smelling incredibly nasty. And that was the moment God called out to him a second time.

When have you benefited from a second chance?

QUESTION #3

God told Jonah to tell the people of Nineveh, "In 40 days Nineveh will be demolished!" Talk about a message that doesn't lend itself to making friends. Can you imagine walking the streets of Chicago or Dallas and yelling, "Your city is about to crumble!"? You might get arrested. You surely wouldn't make any friends. Yet Jonah did what was difficult. It wasn't an easy task, but he was obedient to God and faithful to His message. No doubt it's harder to follow God than to stay in step with this world.

Then something remarkable happened: the people of Nineveh actually responded! They repented of their sins and believed God. To display their repentance, they called for a national fast and put on sackcloth. Even the king of Nineveh repented. He changed from his royal robe into sackcloth to show his own repentance before God (see 3:6). The king charged everyone in Nineveh to call out earnestly before God so that He might change His mind and not overthrow the city (see 3:7-9). God used Jonah's message and obedience to convince the people that He was a righteous God, rightfully and fully capable of destroying them because of their evil ways.

What do God's actions toward Jonah and the Ninevites teach us about His character?

QUESTION #4

Because they believed this about God, the people of Nineveh had the opportunity to discover another part of His character: grace.

Jonah 3:10

The story that weaves through the Book of Jonah is the story of what happens when people respond to what God is calling them to do. This is *exactly* the message we need to hear in order to experience a spiritual awakening.

1. **When we fail to obey God, strong consequences can result from that sin.** Jonah spent three days in the belly of a fish. It could've been worse. He might have drowned when the sailors threw him over the side of that ship. God could have killed him right there in that moment. Instead, God was gracious. Sometimes God brings pain into our lives so that we'll wake up before we bring complete destruction on ourselves.

2. **Blessing is found in obedience.** Even though Jonah didn't know what was going to happen in Nineveh, he was obedient—and God was faithful. The people responded. The king led the people to repentance before God, and the city was saved.

I don't know who originated this statement, but I love its truth: "Someone is waiting for you on the other side of your obedience." A huge city full of dying people was waiting on the other side of Jonah's obedience. If God is burdening your heart to do something, you can be sure He is preparing someone or something to happen on the other side of your obedience.

▶ Do you want to see a spiritual awakening in your family? It starts with your own repentance.

▶ Do you desire for God to start a great revival in your church? Let Him revive your own life.

▶ Do you want God to change your community? Start by letting Him change you.

▶ Groups and communities won't experience renewal and awakening until individuals experience renewal and awakening.

> *How can our group be a safe and supportive place for returning to God?*
>
> **QUESTION #5**

PERSONAL ASSESSMENT: WAKE UP CALL

Take a moment to evaluate your spiritual life. Do you need to wake up?

How consistently do you pray and read the Bible as a daily discipline?

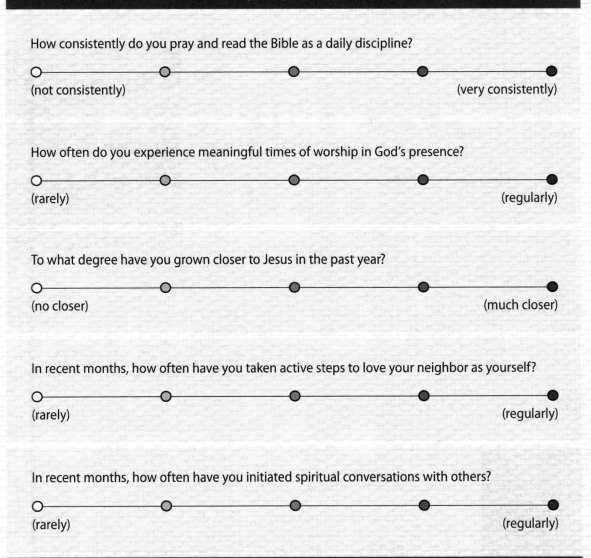

(not consistently)   (very consistently)

How often do you experience meaningful times of worship in God's presence?

(rarely)   (regularly)

To what degree have you grown closer to Jesus in the past year?

(no closer)   (much closer)

In recent months, how often have you taken active steps to love your neighbor as yourself?

(rarely)   (regularly)

In recent months, how often have you initiated spiritual conversations with others?

(rarely)   (regularly)

What would you like to experience on a spiritual level throughout the course of this study?

LIVE IT OUT

How can we be open to God's call and answer when it comes? Consider these suggestions:

▶ **Be sensitive to God's voice.** Don't let yourself become numb toward God. Immerse yourself in Bible study and prayer, asking God to help you be more sensitive to His voice.

▶ **Respond with obedience.** When you hear God telling you to do something in the days to come—do it! Repentance isn't necessary when we obey God's call in the first place.

▶ **Repent when necessary.** None of us will obey perfectly. When you find yourself wandering from God, repent, turn away from your disobedience, and turn back to God.

Spiritual renewal happens as we turn back to God. Be willing to always put your "yes" on the table before Him—even before He asks you to respond.

The Brother of Jesus

"He's the Messiah, no matter what anyone says."

James froze in place: "What?"

Even in the noise of the crowd, his mother spoke loud enough to be heard. "He is the Messiah. I've known that since before He was born."

This was the final blow. "You've believed Him all along."

To continue reading "The Brother of Jesus" from *HomeLife* magazine, visit *BibleStudiesforLife.com/articles*.

My group's prayer requests

_____

_____

_____

_____

_____

_____

_____

_____

_____

My thoughts

SESSION 2

RETURN TO YOUR FIRST LOVE

What hobbies or interests have you lost touch with over the years?

QUESTION **#1**

Return to a love for Christ that permeates everything you do.

THE BIBLE MEETS LIFE

We've all had at least one item we used to cherish that now lies forgotten at the bottom of a closet:

▶ A pair of running shoes from back when you loved to run.

▶ A box full of half-finished craft projects.

▶ A guitar that hasn't been tuned in years.

Losing our enthusiasm for a hobby isn't bad, but it's a whole different matter when we're talking about relationships. Marriages and friendships may start out strong and be bonded with love, but if we're not careful, other things can get in the way. We can get so busy with life that our loved ones get crowded out. We may wake up one day and discover our hearts have strayed. We've lost our love.

But what if we're not talking about a spouse or a friend, but Christ? In Revelation 2, we get a glimpse of a church that had been busy doing many things for God, yet ultimately lost its "first love" for Jesus.

WHAT DOES THE BIBLE SAY?

Revelation 2:1-7 (HCSB)

1 Write to the angel of the church in Ephesus: "The One who holds the seven stars in His right hand and who walks among the seven gold lampstands says:

2 I know your works, your labor, and your endurance, and that you cannot tolerate evil. You have tested those who call themselves apostles and are not, and you have found them to be liars.

3 You also possess endurance and have tolerated many things because of My name and have not grown weary.

4 But I have this against you: You have abandoned the love you had at first.

5 Remember then how far you have fallen; repent, and do the works you did at first. Otherwise, I will come to you and remove your lampstand from its place—unless you repent.

6 Yet you do have this: You hate the practices of the Nicolaitans, which I also hate.

7 "Anyone who has an ear should listen to what the Spirit says to the churches. I will give the victor the right to eat from the tree of life, which is in God's paradise."

Angel of the church (v. 1)—The Greek word for "angel" means "messenger" and can be used either of angelic messengers or human messengers, such as pastors who were responsible for delivering God's message to their churches.

Stars (v. 1)—The seven stars represent the angels (pastors) of the seven churches (see Revelation 1:20).

Gold lampstands (v. 1)—The seven lampstands represent the seven churches in Revelation 2–3.

Nicolaitans (v. 6)—This Nicolaitans were a heretical group in the early church that taught a combination of idolatry and immorality.

Revelation 2:1-4

In the Book of Revelation, God granted John a vision about people and events yet to come (see 1:10-20). Jesus instructed the apostle to write letters to seven churches in Asia Minor, starting with the church at Ephesus. While it appeared Jesus was pleased with everything this church was doing, He had one simple, yet stinging, critique.

First, let's look at all the positive things Jesus pointed out:

1. They worked hard for the Lord, had patient endurance, and did not tolerate evil.

2. They rooted out false prophets.

3. They endured much for Jesus' name without growing weary.

> *How would you compare and contrast doing things for Jesus and spending time with Jesus?*
>
> QUESTION #2

We look at this list and think, "This must be a pretty awesome church." However, the church at Ephesus is a perfect example of the statement: "Good things are the enemy of the best thing." The horrifying statement Jesus made to the church at Ephesus was that, even though they were currently doing many good things, they had abandoned the best thing—their full-hearted love for God.

According to Jesus, the greatest commandment is to "love the Lord your God with all your heart, with all your soul, and with all your mind" (Matt. 22:37). Our love for Jesus is the most important thing about us. We must hold it as tightly as possible.

If you're married, you know "honeymoon love" is like nothing else. When you first get married, the newness and intensity of your love turns everything in your life upside down. But something seems to change over the years. Over time, a spouse may ask, "Why don't you love me like you used to love me?"

> *How can we evaluate whether we've lost our first love for Christ?*
>
> QUESTION #3

This is what Jesus was saying to the church at Ephesus: "I forgave your sin. I changed your life, but your love for Me is not what it used to be. Why don't you love Me like you used to love Me?"

Here's an even tougher question: is Jesus saying the same to you?

FIRST LOVE

Think back to your earliest experiences with Jesus. Use the space below to express how you felt during those experiences. Use any method you prefer to express yourself—draw a picture, make a list of emotions, write out what happened, and so on.

What steps can you take to experience those same emotions in the days to come?

"People do not drift toward holiness. Apart from grace-driven effort, people do not gravitate toward godliness, prayer, obedience to Scripture, faith, and delight in the Lord."

—D. A. CARSON

Revelation 2:5-7

The church at Ephesus may have lost its first love, but Jesus offered them a clear solution. Twice in verse 5 He used the word "repent." On a practical level, to repent means we change the way we're living and adopt a new way. Thinking specifically about salvation, we repent when we surrender our lives to Jesus.

Unfortunately, many Christians don't understand that the word "repent" goes far beyond a one-time experience of repentance before God. To be a healthy follower of Jesus, we must be continually turning our backs to our sin and choosing to live for Him instead. **Repentance is a daily discipline.**

For the church at Ephesus to repent—to turn back—meant they would "do the works you did at first" (v. 5). Jesus called them to do whatever it was in the beginning of their spiritual walks that led them to such a strong relationship with Him.

What's more, Jesus laid out a condition in verse 5. If the church refused to repent, He would come and remove their lampstand from its place. When you blow a candle out, the candle loses its ability to give light—to have influence over the darkness. If the church at Ephesus did not repent and return to a love for Jesus, He would remove their influence.

Verse 7 is essential to the entire process of returning to your love for Jesus. Jesus has given us the key to the entire process, and it's not what we typically think. Here's the key: "Listen."

The whole process of repentance and renewal cannot begin to happen if you don't listen. Jesus said, "Anyone who has an ear should listen to what the Spirit says to the churches" (v. 7). In other words: listen up, everybody!

> **What does it look like for a follower of Christ to repent?**
>
> QUESTION #4

What did the Spirit say to the church at Ephesus—and to us? Listen and hear these three words:

1. **Remember.** Think about the healthiest and most-productive seasons in your spiritual life. If you find yourself at a place where your love for Jesus has waned, return to the things that were present when you were walking closely with God.

2. **Repent.** Anything, no matter how good, that keeps you from your love for Jesus is a sin. Surrender these things before Jesus and watch Him begin to move in your life once more.

3. **Return.** At the heart of Jesus' message is a loving call: "Return to Me." As we turn from sin, we turn toward Jesus. We simply must return to Jesus.

How do we get love and passion for Jesus back to where it needs to be in our church? We must return to Jesus. When we return to Jesus, we will regain a love that truly does permeate everything we do.

It's a simple formula, really. When our love for Jesus is wrong, nothing is right. But when our love for Jesus is right, He makes everything else right!

> *How do we train ourselves to listen to God's Spirit throughout the day?*

QUESTION #5

LIVE IT OUT

How do we return to our first love? Consider the following suggestions as you follow Christ in the days to come:

▶ **Remember.** Write down the top three things that describe your Christian walk at its most healthy.

▶ **Repent.** Spend time identifying any habits or patterns in your life that are detrimental to your love for Jesus. Repent right now before God. Turn from those sins today.

▶ **Return.** Write down a practical plan for drawing closer to God. This may be a renewed commitment to daily Bible reading, prayer, sharing your faith, and so on.

The wonderful thing about the grace of Jesus is that it doesn't matter where we've been or what we've done—His grace is greater than all our sin. Throw yourself into the loving arms of Jesus and watch Him bring back your love for Him.

Afloat and Alone

Pay attention, because if you're not paying active attention, you're going to drift. And if you drift, it's always going to be away from Jesus, not toward Him.

To continue reading "Afloat and Alone" from *HomeLife* magazine, visit *BibleStudiesforLife.com/articles*.

My group's prayer requests

....

....

....

....

....

....

....

....

....

....

My thoughts

SESSION 3

RETURN TO PRAYER

How do you typically respond to bad news?

QUESTION #1

Move forward by retreating into prayer.

THE BIBLE MEETS LIFE

It's staring right at you:

▶ The warning light on your car's dashboard.

▶ The unopened bill.

▶ The calendar reminder to make a doctor's appointment.

You know what you need to do, but you don't want to take the next step. Why? Because you know it's likely to be bad news.

We can try to avoid bad news—pretend it's not there. But that doesn't change reality. We have to face up to bad news when it comes. The key question is: how do we face an onslaught of bad news?

That's what Nehemiah was faced with in today's Scripture: a mountain of bad news that hit him like a truck. Fortunately, Nehemiah responded by turning to God in prayer. His example can help us do the same.

WHAT DOES THE BIBLE SAY?

Nehemiah 1:3-10 (HCSB)

3 They said to me, "The remnant in the province, who survived the exile, are in great trouble and disgrace. Jerusalem's wall has been broken down, and its gates have been burned down."

4 When I heard these words, I sat down and wept. I mourned for a number of days, fasting and praying before the God of heaven.

5 I said, Yahweh, the God of heaven, the great and awe-inspiring God who keeps His gracious covenant with those who love Him and keep His commands,

6 let Your eyes be open and Your ears be attentive to hear Your servant's prayer that I now pray to You day and night for Your servants, the Israelites. I confess the sins we have committed against You. Both I and my father's house have sinned.

7 We have acted corruptly toward You and have not kept the commands, statutes, and ordinances You gave Your servant Moses.

8 Please remember what You commanded Your servant Moses: "If you are unfaithful, I will scatter you among the peoples.

9 But if you return to Me and carefully observe My commands, even though your exiles were banished to the ends of the earth, I will gather them from there and bring them to the place where I chose to have My name dwell."

10 They are Your servants and Your people. You redeemed them by Your great power and strong hand."

Exile (v. 3)—In 586 B.C., the Southern Kingdom of Judah fell to the Babylonian armies. As a result, the Jews were deported, or exiled, to Babylon.

Remnant (v. 3)—This term refers to the Jews who survived the Babylonian captivity and returned at the decree of Cyrus in 538 B.C. to reestablish life in Jerusalem and Judah.

Redeemed (v. 10)—To redeem involves paying a price to release a person from slavery. The reference here may denote God's bringing His people out of slavery in Egypt during the time of Moses; it also indicates the return of the Jews to Judah following the Babylonian exile.

Nehemiah 1:3

After 70 years of captivity in Babylon, the people of Israel were allowed to return to their homeland, including Jerusalem, in 538 B.C. Around 90 years later, a man named Nehemiah, still living in Babylon, asked his brother Hanani about the condition of Jerusalem and those who had returned to live there. The report he received was grim: the people were in trouble, the wall around Jerusalem had been broken down, and its gates were destroyed.

Nehemiah was stunned. No walls and no gates meant the residents of Jerusalem were completely unprotected. They were vulnerable to any number of threats. Why would God allow this to happen? After all, these were His chosen people, and He had promised they would return to their own land and prosper after the exile (see Jer. 29:10-11,14). But God also said: "You will call to Me and come and pray to Me, and I will listen to you. You will seek Me and find Me when you search for Me with all your heart" (vv. 12-13).

God wants a relationship with us. To accomplish that goal, He often moves in our lives in one of two ways:

1. He moves in response to our desperation for Him.

2. He allows trouble in our lives because He knows that will bring us to desperation for Him.

When I think about that word "desperation," I think about growing up in south Texas. The summers there are boiling hot, and I think about going outside to play as a child. I often took no water with me, and in the scorching afternoon heat I would suddenly realize I was thirsty. To ignore that thirst and keep playing would eventually lead to dizziness, nausea, and even a loss of consciousness. At some point, I would become *desperate* for water and hydration.

In a similar way, we can deceive ourselves into thinking our spiritual lives are fine—even when we have no intimate walk with Jesus, no fellowship with others, and no sense of being on mission to make disciples. The reality is that we need the refreshing water of God's presence in our lives.

God's people were in a desperate situation, and Nehemiah knew it. Fortunately, the desperate situation moved Nehemiah to desperately seek God.

> *What are some symptoms of spiritual trouble in today's culture?*

QUESTION #2

LOCATION, LOCATION, LOCATION

Circle the image below that best reflects your favorite environment for connecting with God in prayer.

What steps can you take to increase the amount of time you spend in prayer each day?

Nehemiah 1:4-6a

Hearing the plight of God's people and Jerusalem humbled Nehemiah. He was so broken at the news that he sat down before the Lord for days in order to mourn, pray, and fast. He allowed the devastation of his people to drive his desperation to see God move.

It's interesting that the first words of Nehemiah's recorded prayer weren't focused on the bad news he had received. Instead, Nehemiah began by focusing on who God is—by throwing himself on the foundation of God's character. Standing on the truth of that foundation, Nehemiah prayed that God would listen to his prayer and respond with compassion.

In the same way, our hope for moving forward spiritually isn't based on overcoming our problems, but on the simple fact of who God is. If you find yourself in a place of devastation and desperation, consider the character of God and surrender to Him. This is the path to spiritual renewal and awakening.

I admit this can be difficult.

When we see a problem or encounter a crisis, our first response typically is to try and fix it ourselves. Nehemiah did the opposite by retreating into prayer and fasting. By turning away from his problems, Nehemiah sought the ultimate solution to those problems. The reality is that retreating into prayer is actually the best way to move forward. **Prayer should be our first response, not our last resort. When we seek God in prayer and fasting, He responds.**

"Fasting is abstaining from food with a spiritual goal in mind. When we fast, we're willing to give up the most natural thing our body desires—namely, food—in order to beg the God of heaven to do something supernatural in our lives."

—RONNIE FLOYD

> *Nehemiah responded with mourning, praying, and fasting. When should we incorporate these practices in our lives?*
>
> QUESTION #3

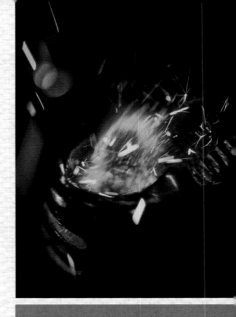

Nehemiah 1:6b-10

As Nehemiah contemplated the circumstances of his people, he knew they must deal with their sin. Repentance was the only answer. It's interesting that Nehemiah included himself as part of the problem. He wasn't living in Jerusalem, yet he counted himself and his family among those who had sinned against God. Nehemiah sought restoration for his fellow Jews, but he began with himself. That's important.

Before God brings revival to a nation or group of people, He brings it first into the hearts of individuals. One person's confession and repentance can be the spark that ignites a great awakening. Nehemiah was that spark for the Jews in Jerusalem. God burdened Nehemiah about his own condition, and He used Nehemiah to rebuild and restore.

In September 1857, God used another spark by the name of Jeremiah Lanphier. He was a businessman so burdened to see God move that He began a prayer meeting in Manhattan. While it started out small—the first meeting only had six in attendance—God began a wave of prayer and renewal that led to the revival of 1858. More than one million people were converted to faith in Christ in one year.[1]

Can you imagine what would happen if that kind of movement happened in your community today? In our country? Millions would come to Christ! And it all starts with prayer. You never know how God will use the spark of one desperate, praying believer to influence another person, who influences others, who influences others—until millions of lives are changed to the glory of God. Be that spark.

> **What role should confession play in our lives?**
>
> QUESTION #4

> **What's one step you could take to improve your prayer life?**
>
> QUESTION #5

LIVE IT OUT

How will you move forward with God this week? Consider the following suggestions:

▶ **Pray every day.** Stop trying to fix your problems on your own and take your problems to the only One who can really solve them.

▶ **Schedule time for uninterrupted prayer.** Block out at least 15-30 minutes for longer experiences with prayer. Guard that time and use it to focus on God as you pray for revival for yourself, your family, your church, and your community.

▶ **Fast.** Fasting can take your prayer life to a new level. Consider fasting as a group on a particular day.

We all receive bad news, but there is a way to deal with it: pray. There has never been a great movement of God that was not preceded by the extraordinary prayer of God's people.

Fasting and Prayer as Spiritual Worship

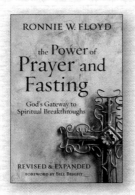

The disciplines of prayer and fasting are not reduced to a formula or a hoop that we are to jump through as if we are in a kind of spiritual circus. Nor are they physical tests or exercises in mental discipline. True prayer and fasting are attitudes of the heart and cries of the soul.

To continue reading this excerpt from *The Power of Prayer and Fasting*, by Ronnie Floyd, visit *BibleStudiesforLife.com/articles*.

My group's prayer requests

_____
_____
_____
_____
_____
_____
_____
_____
_____
_____

My thoughts

1. "Revival Born in a Prayer Meeting," _Christian Life_ magazine; source: _cslewisinstitute.org_ (Accessed on November 13, 2014).

SESSION 4

RETURN TO GOD'S WORD

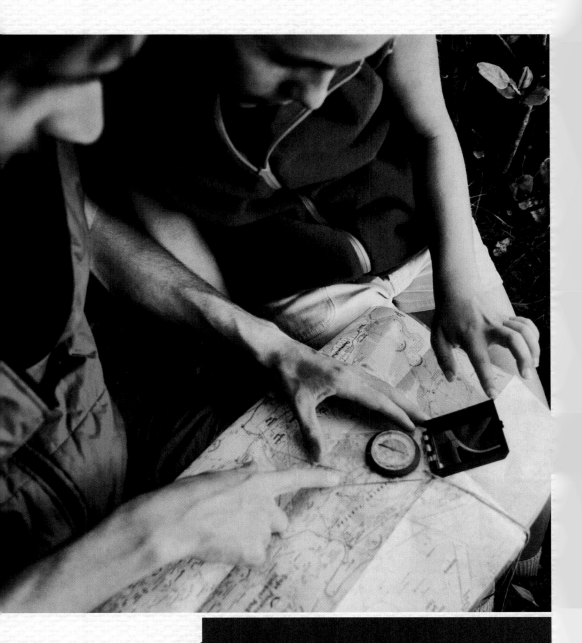

When has following someone's directions taken you someplace unexpected?

QUESTION #1

God's Word is the fuel for a consistent lifestyle.

THE BIBLE MEETS LIFE

Remember road maps? We used to unfold a huge map, pinpoint our destination, and follow the snarl of roads and turns until we got there. Then came the hard part: folding up the map afterward.

Now most of us rely on GPS. Just type in the desired destination, and the GPS or phone app leads us right to where we want to go. The app will even give verbal instructions, reminding us when and what direction to turn—or when to make a U-turn to get back on course.

Life is so much easier now. Or is it?

Our phones can still go dead, or we can drive into an area of bad cell service. And even like the old-school maps, the GPS may not be updated with new or changing roads. We can still get lost.

Thankfully, God gave us a different kind of road map for life—one that never fails. This map, His Word, gives us His directions on how to live and is our fuel for spiritual renewal. The Israelites knew this in the days of Nehemiah, and it's a truth we should hold onto today.

WHAT DOES THE BIBLE SAY?

Nehemiah 8:1-8 (HCSB)

1 All the people gathered together at the square in front of the Water Gate. They asked Ezra the scribe to bring the book of the law of Moses that the LORD had given Israel.

2 On the first day of the seventh month, Ezra the priest brought the law before the assembly of men, women, and all who could listen with understanding.

3 While he was facing the square in front of the Water Gate, he read out of it from daybreak until noon before the men, the women, and those who could understand. All the people listened attentively to the book of the law.

4 Ezra the scribe stood on a high wooden platform made for this purpose. Mattithiah, Shema, Anaiah, Uriah, Hilkiah, and Maaseiah stood beside him on his right; to his left were Pedaiah, Mishael, Malchijah, Hashum, Hash-baddanah, Zechariah, and Meshullam.

5 Ezra opened the book in full view of all the people, since he was elevated above everyone. As he opened it, all the people stood up.

6 Ezra praised the LORD, the great God, and with their hands uplifted all the people said, "Amen, Amen!" Then they bowed down and worshiped the LORD with their faces to the ground.

7 Jeshua, Bani, Sherebiah, Jamin, Akkub, Shabbethai, Hodiah, Maaseiah, Kelita, Azariah, Jozabad, Hanan, and Pelaiah, who were Levites, explained the law to the people as they stood in their places.

8 They read out of the book of the law of God, translating and giving the meaning so that the people could understand what was read.

Water Gate (v. 1)—This refers to the gate in the wall of Jerusalem leading to the Gihon Spring. It was not the same as the Water Gate in Herod's temple, which did not exist at this time. Since this spring provided the main water source outside the wall, it was a gathering point for the community.

Amen (v. 6)—"Amen" is an expression of support or confirmation, coming from the verb that means "to confirm," "to support," or "to uphold." As a congregational response, the word was an affirmation of the truthfulness of a spoken prayer, praise, or teaching.

Nehemiah 8:1-3

God sent Nehemiah to Jerusalem to help His people restore their city from the outside in. Through the work and ministry of both Nehemiah and Ezra the priest, the Israelites not only rebuilt the walls and the city, but their lives as well.

In Nehemiah 8, the Jewish people gathered to celebrate all that had happened. Actually, this was more than a celebration; it was a time of rededication. The gathering occurred in the seventh month of the year, which is significant because the Jews celebrated three events during that month: the Feast of Trumpets, the Day of Atonement, and the Feast of Booths (see Lev. 23:23-43). Every seven years during the Feast of Booths, God's Word was to be read before His people (see Deut. 31:10-13).

The Jews of Nehemiah's time had recaptured the significance of their festivals and realized the importance of "the book of the law of Moses" (v. 1). They were hungry to hear what God had to say, which meant:

1. **They were dedicated to listening to the Word of God.** The people listened to Ezra and others read and explain the Word of God from early in the morning until midday. In other words, they listened to the Word of God for six hours!

2. **They were attentive to the Word of God.** To be attentive means to concentrate, be observant, and be focused. The people's hearts and minds were not fixed on simply listening to the words, but on retaining the truth from the law being read and explained to them.

Since God's Word really is the fuel for sustained restoration in our lives, we must give it the priority it deserves. Let's be people who have such a hunger for God that our lives overflow with dedication and attentiveness to His Word.

> *How do our circumstances impact the way we approach the Bible?*
>
> **QUESTION #2**

FUEL STOP

The Bible offers needed fuel for our spiritual lives. Therefore, think of ways you could incorporate God's Word into the different phases of your day.
Choose two phases from the list below and record your thoughts. Be creative!

Working   **Relaxing**   **Driving**   **Resting**

What obstacles prevent you from incorporating these ideas into your day more regularly?

Nehemiah 8:4-6

As the Jews gathered to hear Ezra read, they showed great honor and respect for the Scriptures. "As he opened it, all the people stood up" (v. 5). Ezra didn't have to ask the people to stand; it was likely a customary act of honor, even submission. We see the same thing today when a bride walks down the aisle at her wedding—the congregation stands in honor. When the president of the United States enters a room, the people stand in honor. When we sing the national anthem, we stand in honor of our country. We stand as a way of expressing the worth of a person or event.

When the people of God stood to receive the Word of God, they were publicly displaying their belief that what was happening—hearing the Word of God—was important.

When Ezra opened the book, he was moved to praise God, and all the people responded with worship: "With their hands uplifted all the people said, 'Amen Amen!'" (v. 6). This was a declaration of worship and submission to the authority of Scripture. What a wonderful picture of God's people responding to God's Word! The Israelites were deeply moved as they heard and understood the words of the law.

Responding to God's Word is one of the greatest pathways to spiritual renewal. As we renew our walk with God and experience personal revival, God's Word is the fuel that sustains us and keeps us spiritually moving forward. I'm not talking about a quick, momentary response to God's Word that fades after a while. We need a consistent lifestyle of sensitivity before God. His Word holds us accountable.

To return to our previous metaphor, the Bible is the map that keeps us on the path of renewal and revival. When we stray, it holds us accountable and shows us the way back.

> *What's the connection between engaging the Bible and worshiping God?*

QUESTION #3

Nehemiah 8:7-8

The men mentioned in verse 7 were Levites, and their task that day was to help the people understand the law. Therefore, in verse 8, the Levites did two things to carry out this task:

1. **Reading and translating.** The people had been in captivity in a foreign land and culture for decades. There was a culture gap, and many of the people may have even lost their ability to read, speak, and understand Hebrew. It's quite possible these Levites were translating the Scriptures into the language and vernacular of the people.

2. **Giving the meaning.** The Levites were actively pursuing clarity and understanding. Clarity is important in all communication, but doubly so when we're reading and studying the Bible.

In bringing God's Word to the people, the Levites surely offered practical application, as well. "Now here's what you do with this truth." When we read the Bible for our own personal growth, we need to continually ask ourselves what we must do as a result. We must learn to apply the Word. In addition, as you apply specific passages of God's Word to your own life, tell others about it. You can only teach what you know, so focus on your own study and application of God's Word as you help others follow Him.

Learning the Word of God is like eating an elephant. It's a huge task, but you only have to take one bite at a time. Start eating and enjoy a lifetime of feasting upon God's Word! As you do, your walk with Christ will be a consistent witness pointing directly to Him.

When have you recently been affected or convicted by your study of God's Word?

QUESTION #4

What steps can you take to better understand and apply God's Word?

QUESTION #5

LIVE IT OUT

How can you make sure the Scriptures have their rightful place in your life? Consider the following:

▶ **Read up.** Make a habit of reading the Bible every day. A devotional book or magazine can help you get started, but give God uninterrupted time to speak through His Word.

▶ **Listen up.** Make yourself more attentive to God's Word by taking notes. Write down what you hear God saying to you.

▶ **Step up.** Lead a small group or Bible study. Teach children or students at your church. The greatest way to learn the Scriptures is to teach them to someone else!

We have plenty of tools to give us direction on a physical level. But God's Word is the only thing that can give us the proper spiritual direction we need in life. It truly is our only foundation and fuel to sustain a renewed walk with Christ.

Great Is God's Faithfulness

"My story is not about a man's faithfulness to God; it's about God's faithfulness to a man." **These are the words of speaker, author, and pastor of Providence Church in Frisco, Texas, Afshin Ziafat. Afshin's story began in Houston in a well-to-do Muslim-Iranian family. When Afshin was 2, he and his family moved back to Tehran. A few years later, the Islamic revolution erupted, and intense fighting broke out in Iran, so Afshin's father decided it was best to bring his family back to the United States. Afshin was 6. Their reception upon returning to Houston wasn't a warm one.**

To continue reading "Great Is God's Faithfulness" from *HomeLife* magazine, visit *BibleStudiesforLife.com/articles*.

My group's prayer requests

....

....

....

....

....

....

....

....

....

....

My thoughts

SESSION 5

RETURN TO UNITY

When have you felt united with others in a common cause?

QUESTION **#1**

#Awake

Walking with Christ brings us together in unity and purpose.

THE BIBLE MEETS LIFE

It's interesting to see what can bring people together:

▶ Two men can be polar opposites, but they'll sit side-by-side and high-five each other during a football game.

▶ Total strangers often start talking to each other when a canceled flight leaves them stranded together at a gate.

▶ During a national tragedy, citizens come together in extraordinary ways.

The church takes unity to an entirely different level. The church is diverse—white collar and blue collar, Republican and Democrat, plus every ethnic group under the sun—yet we come together because of our shared faith in Jesus Christ. At least, we're supposed to come together. Sometimes our differences still get in the way.

In the Book of Acts, Luke described a very young church that did more than talk about unity in Christ. They lived it.

WHAT DOES THE BIBLE SAY?

Acts 4:31-37 *(HCSB)*

31 When they had prayed, the place where they were assembled was shaken, and they were all filled with the Holy Spirit and began to speak God's message with boldness.

32 Now the large group of those who believed were of one heart and mind, and no one said that any of his possessions was his own, but instead they held everything in common.

33 And the apostles were giving testimony with great power to the resurrection of the Lord Jesus, and great grace was on all of them.

34 For there was not a needy person among them, because all those who owned lands or houses sold them, brought the proceeds of the things that were sold,

35 and laid them at the apostles' feet. This was then distributed for each person's basic needs.

36 Joseph, a Levite and a Cypriot by birth, the one the apostles called Barnabas, which is translated Son of Encouragement,

37 sold a field he owned, brought the money, and laid it at the apostles' feet.

Boldness (v. 31)—The disciples had previously prayed that God would enable them to speak the truth with boldness in spite of the threats against them (see 4:29). God directly answered their prayer with a demonstration of His power.

Acts 4:31

There's a lot that leads up to Acts 4:31. For starters, the religious authorities had arrested Peter and John for preaching about Jesus' resurrection. When the two apostles were brought before the rulers, they gave a bold declaration of their faith in Christ. They boldly spoke of Jesus as the only way to salvation (see 4:1-12). The authorities charged them not to speak about Jesus anymore, but the apostles said, "We are unable to stop speaking about what we have seen and heard" (v. 20).

After Peter and John were released, they went straight to the believers and told them all that had happened. The believers responded with an amazing prayer: "And now, Lord, consider their threats, and grant that Your slaves may speak Your message with complete boldness" (v. 29). They didn't ask God to deliver them from the hands of those who would harm them. They didn't even pray for protection. Their only prayer was that God would help them be bold in the face of persecution.

These early believers were facing the pressure of persecution, but they didn't run. Instead, they came together. What united them? Their faith in Christ and their desire to spread the good news of the gospel to all who needed to hear it.

As the believers expressed this unity in their prayer, three amazing things happened:

1. The place where they were meeting was shaken.

2. They were all filled with the Holy Spirit.

3. They began to speak God's message with boldness.

> **What factors help people feel united?**
>
> QUESTION #2

UNITY AND DIVERSITY

Male   Child   Black/African American   Married   Young Adult

Full-time Employee   Female   White/Caucasian   Widowed   Teen

Asian/Pacific Islander   Part-time Employee   Single   Senior

Unemployed   Hispanic/Latino   Divorced   Adult

What are some common beliefs and principles that unite these different groups in your congregation and community?

"Finally, brothers, rejoice. Become mature, be encouraged, be of the same mind, be at peace, and the God of love and peace will be with you."

—2 CORINTHIANS 13:11

Acts 4:32-33

When individual believers are filled with God's Holy Spirit, they can't help uniting with one another. The Spirit makes all the difference. When the Holy Spirit gets involved with individuals, a church, a community, or a nation, He will produce change—and it will be change that lasts.

The early believers were deeply impacted by what the Holy Spirit had done and was doing in their lives. Throughout the remaining verses of Acts 4, we can see how the Spirit's unifying presence manifested itself among these believers. Specifically, they "were of one heart and mind" (v. 32). These two mindsets were foundational elements of their early ministry:

1. **They were one in heart with a mutual generosity.** The early believers shared their possessions. It's rare to see this kind of radical generosity today. We may contribute to a fund, but what these believers did is comparable to discovering a fellow believer who needs transportation and giving him your car. One person's needs became everyone's needs. That's some serious unity!

2. **They were one in mind and purpose.** They prayed for boldness to proclaim the message of Jesus, and God answered their prayer. The apostles continued to preach boldly and with power about the gospel. This was their one mission. We can do a lot of "good things," but we must have unity on "the main thing"—preaching the gospel to every man, woman, boy, and girl around the world.

A time is coming when people from every nation, tribe, and language will gather around the throne of God and give praise and glory to Him. God is at work around the world bringing these people to Himself. Our mission is to join Him in that task.

> *How have you seen mutual generosity impact your church or community?*
>
> QUESTION #3

Acts 4:34-37

The Holy Spirit leads us to surrender, which is why the believers in the early church willingly gave up their possessions for one another. They joyfully let go of everything else so they could fully embrace Christ and focus completely on Him and His gospel.

Surrender is often hard, but it shouldn't be. When we surrender to the Holy Spirit, we gain far more than we give up. When we surrender to the Lord, we surrender in victory, not defeat!

▶ Every time He convicts us of sin, it's time to surrender that sin to God and experience His forgiveness, freedom, and grace (see 1 John 1:9).

▶ Every time He calls us to respond generously to a need, we can joyfully let go of what we know was never "ours" in the first place.

▶ Every time He speaks to us about the direction and purpose of our lives, we can surrender and join Him in the great adventure of His mission.

Verses 36-37 give us a specific example of one believer's generosity. Barnabas sold a field and brought the proceeds to the apostles for distribution. We'll look more closely at Barnabas's mission and work in our next session. For now, however, let's note how Barnabas surrendered his life, exemplifying the mindsets noted earlier in verses 32-33:

▶ We know Barnabas was "of one heart" with his fellow Christians because of his generosity.

▶ We know Barnabas was "of one mind" with his fellow Christians because of his encouragement and his laser-like focus on the church's mission.

Barnabas surrendered himself to the Lord. His devotion to Christ was apparent because of his devotion to and unity with other believers. Choose to be a Barnabas in your church.

> *What's your initial reaction to these verses?*
>
> QUESTION #4

> *How should these verses guide our actions and attitudes today?*
>
> QUESTION #5

LIVE IT OUT

There is incredible power when God unites His people. How will you strive for unity of heart and mind within your church community?

▶ **Yield.** Surrender yourself each morning to the lordship of Christ and let Him fill you with His Holy Spirit.

▶ **Pray.** Pray daily for unity in your church and among believers in your community. Ask God to remove all barriers to unity and make your church family one in heart and mind.

▶ **Share.** Take a bold step to confirm that you've surrendered everything to Christ. When you see someone with a need this week, do whatever you can do to take care of it.

God uses our unity in Him to bring revival to our lives and churches—and that leads to spiritual awakening in our nation. May God through His Holy Spirit impact you in such a way that unity abounds in your family, church, and community.

Common Ground

I don't belong here. *That was my first thought when I walked into the room labeled, "Singles." I had recently relocated and was interested in building relationships in my new church home. On that particular Sunday morning, I was greeted at the church entrance and asked what kind of class I wanted to attend. After a short discussion, the greeter led me to a small classroom upstairs. To be honest, I felt like I'd been dropped off in the "lost and found" box for Christians. Other than being single, I thought,* **What else could I possibly have in common with these people?**

To continue reading "Common Ground" from *HomeLife* magazine, visit *BibleStudiesforLife.com/articles*.

My group's prayer requests

My thoughts

SESSION 6

RETURN TO THE TASK

Where do you like to go to recharge your batteries?

QUESTION #1

THE POINT

A revitalized church spreads the gospel.

THE BIBLE MEETS LIFE

Sometimes you just need to get away, don't you? There's something magical about a vacation.

And I'm not talking about one of those vacations where you're on the move nonstop and everything is more work than relaxation. We've all experienced "vacations" where we came home more exhausted than when we left.

What you really need is a break from the routine. Something that helps you refresh your body and spirit. Something that refocuses your mind and emotions. Doesn't that sound inviting?

Here's the good news: two of the most powerful ways to do that—to regain focus—don't even require leaving town! Prayer and fasting can be done right where you are, and they can revitalize you and lead you to fix your attention on the parts of life that are truly important. In Acts 13, we see this principle at work in the church at Antioch. They prayed. They fasted. And God did something incredible in their midst.

WHAT DOES THE BIBLE SAY?

Acts 13:1-3,44-52 (HCSB)

1 In the church that was at Antioch there were prophets and teachers: Barnabas, Simeon who was called Niger, Lucius the Cyrenian, Manaen, a close friend of Herod the tetrarch, and Saul.

2 As they were ministering to the Lord and fasting, the Holy Spirit said, "Set apart for Me Barnabas and Saul for the work I have called them to."

3 Then after they had fasted, prayed, and laid hands on them, they sent them off.

44 The following Sabbath almost the whole town assembled to hear the message of the Lord.

45 But when the Jews saw the crowds, they were filled with jealousy and began to oppose what Paul was saying by insulting him.

46 Then Paul and Barnabas boldly said: "It was necessary that God's message be spoken to you first. But since you reject it and consider yourselves unworthy of eternal life, we now turn to the Gentiles!

47 For this is what the Lord has commanded us: I have made you a light for the Gentiles to bring salvation to the ends of the earth."

48 When the Gentiles heard this, they rejoiced and glorified the message of the Lord, and all who had been appointed to eternal life believed.

49 So the message of the Lord spread through the whole region.

50 But the Jews incited the prominent women, who worshiped God, and the leading men of the city. They stirred up persecution against Paul and Barnabas and expelled them from their district.

51 But they shook the dust off their feet against them and went to Iconium.

52 And the disciples were filled with joy and the Holy Spirit.

Ministering to the Lord (v. 2)—This phrase literally means "serving the Lord." In the Old Testament, it referred to priests and Levites carrying out their duties in the temple. Our English word "liturgy" is derived from this Greek term.

Laid hands (v. 3)—This was a symbolic and ceremonial act of recognizing a divine call, separating for a designated task, and invoking divine blessing.

Gentiles (v. 46)—This term referred to people who were not Jewish by birth. Synonyms of this term include "nations" and "pagans."

Acts 13:1-3

The church in Antioch is a great example of believers who loved Jesus and reflected that love in their ministry to people. They gladly shared the gospel with anyone—even Gentiles (see 11:20). Up to that time, Christianity was considered an extension of Jewish beliefs. After all, Jesus Himself said He had come to fulfill everything the Jews believed (see Matt. 5:17). Therefore, Jews who became Christians naturally went to other Jews to share the gospel.

In Antioch, however, believers began to realize the message of Christ benefited all people. They spread that message among the Gentiles, and "the Lord's hand was with them, and a large number who believed turned to the Lord" (Acts 11:21). With that, the church in Antioch caught a passion for missions.

When we come to Acts 13, the Christians in Antioch were worshiping the Lord and fasting. Many scholars believe this time of worship, prayer, and fasting was undertaken with a specific goal in mind. The church had a heart for evangelism and missions, but how were they to proceed? What were they supposed to do? Instead of coming up with a plan that seemed best to them, the Christians at Antioch stopped. They prayed and fasted. They fixed their hearts completely on God.

And God responded! When the church's full and undivided attention was on the Lord, the Holy Spirit answered and offered direction. Specifically, the Spirit said, "Set apart for Me Barnabas and Saul for the work I have called them to" (v. 2). This was a critically important moment in the early stages of Christianity. The church at Antioch had gotten serious before God, and they were about to get serious about the Great Commission (see Matt. 28:19-20).

> **What can we do to intentionally seek God's guidance?**
>
> QUESTION #2

> **What do these verses teach about the process of sharing the gospel?**

QUESTION **#3**

Acts 13:44-47

Saul (also known as the apostle Paul) and Barnabas headed first to the island of Cyprus. After going through the whole island, they crossed over to Asia and came to a place known as Antioch in Pisidia. They entered the synagogue on the Sabbath day, and Paul spoke to those gathered there. He preached about the connection between God's work in the Old Testament and His work through Jesus. Many responded positively to the gospel message (see Acts 13:43).

Not everybody was enthusiastic about Paul's preaching, however. When just about all the people in the city showed up the next Sabbath day to hear Paul preach about Jesus, some of the Jews "were filled with jealousy and began to oppose what Paul was saying by insulting him" (v. 45).

This is a principle: whenever God is working, we can fully expect Satan to fight against that work. "For our battle is not against flesh and blood, but against the rulers, against the authorities, against the world powers of this darkness, against the spiritual forces of evil in the heavens" (Eph. 6:12). Satan will do everything in his power to stop the church from praying and advancing the gospel.

Unfortunately, Satan sometimes succeeds in his efforts. We've all heard of churches undone by disunity, gossip, immorality, and myriad other sins. Satan prowls around like a lion, seeking someone to devour (see 1 Pet. 5:8). Churches that fall prey to Satan's attacks don't resist him and stand firm. They cease to be praying churches, centered on the gospel and fixed solely on Christ.

Yet when Satan raises his ugly head even today, we must continue to march on. We must not back down from our call to the Great Commission. Paul and Barnabas did not. They didn't soften their message one bit. If anything, they become even bolder in their approach. What an example for us!

"Can we follow the Savior far, who have no wound or scar?"

—AMY CARMICHAEL

Acts 13:48-52

In spite of Satan's efforts, Jesus still does amazing things among His people. The Jews may have rejected the gospel, but the Gentiles responded joyfully with open and ready hearts. They rejoiced and glorified God. Many believed and were saved. In spite of opposition and even persecution, the word of the Lord continued to spread throughout the whole region.

Persecution cannot stop the gospel from spreading. In fact, many times it does just the opposite. It's like different people I've known who try to get a campfire started "the old-fashioned way." I've seen them spend hours striking a flint or rubbing sticks together with no results. Sooner or later somebody brings over a can of gasoline, and then—woosh! The fire has a sudden and fierce awakening.

Persecution can be like that gasoline. It can cause an explosive spread of the gospel. Missionaries often speak about amazing ministry opportunities in places of intense persecution—places where God is doing a great work.

How did Paul and Barnabas respond to persecution? They went right on preaching (see vv. 50-51). They went to the next city and strolled into the synagogue. They kept up the same routine throughout the Book of Acts—proclaiming the gospel, harvesting spiritual fruit, undergoing persecution, and then moving someplace new to proclaim the gospel once again.

Don't lose sight of what God was doing. The Gentile believers rejoiced in God's salvation. These new disciples "were filled with joy and the Holy Spirit" (v. 52), which surely brought joy to Paul and Barnabas as well. As Paul later wrote to a different group of Gentiles in Philippi: "I give thanks to my God for every remembrance of you, always praying with joy for all of you in my every prayer" (Phil. 1:3-4). **We can find no greater joy than walking in the Spirit while being obedient to the call of God.**

> *How have you experienced resistance in your attempts to make disciples?*
>
> QUESTION **#4**

> *What steps can we take to strive for revival in our church and community?*
>
> QUESTION **#5**

THE SPARK OF PERSECUTION

Using the map below, mark an X on the different countries or regions where you know Christians are actively persecuted today.

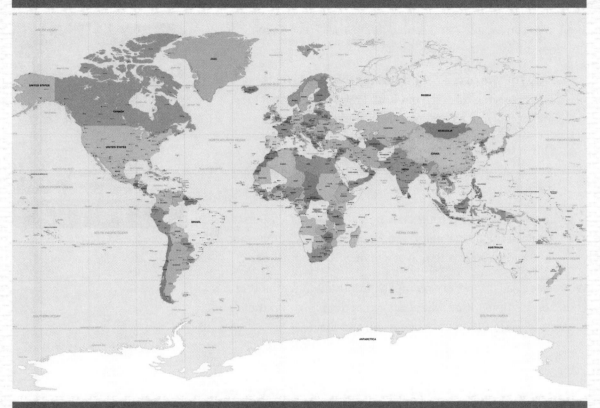

What steps can you (and your group) take to support persecuted Christians around the world?

LIVE IT OUT

How will you obey God's call to fulfill the Great Commission? Consider the following suggestions:

▶ **Pray for the lost every day.** Pray specifically for someone who needs the message of Christ. Pray for the gospel to advance in your community and around the world.

▶ **Share the gospel.** Spreading the gospel isn't just for pastors and preachers. Actively seek out opportunities to share the good news of Christ.

▶ **Lead your group on mission.** Make plans as a group to proclaim the gospel in a tangible, practical way within your community. Start with prayer and move out from there.

We've seen what we can accomplish in our own lives and in our churches. It's time to see what God can accomplish. And there's no better way to start than through fasting and prayer.

Students Standing Strong

My husband, Jay, and I live in Grapevine, Texas. We have five incredible kids. Our parenting journey began with a few goals: when our children leave home, they'll have a personal relationship with Christ, they'll be filled with His Spirit, they will desire to live according to His Word, and they will know they're unconditionally loved by their parents and God. But achieving goals requires an action plan.

To continue reading "Students Standing Strong" from *HomeLife* magazine, visit *BibleStudiesforLife.com/articles*.

My group's prayer requests

_____

_____

_____

_____

_____

_____

_____

_____

_____

_____

My thoughts

LEADER GUIDE

AWAKE

GENERAL INSTRUCTIONS

In order to make the most of this study and to ensure a richer group experience, it's recommended that all group participants read through the teaching and discussion content in full before each group meeting. As a leader, it is also a good idea for you to be familiar with this content and prepared to summarize it for your group members as you move through the material each week.

Each session of the Bible study is made up of three sections:

1. THE BIBLE MEETS LIFE.

An introduction to the theme of the session and its connection to everyday life, along with a brief overview of the primary Scripture text. This section also includes an icebreaker question or activity.

2. WHAT DOES THE BIBLE SAY?

This comprises the bulk of each session and includes the primary Scripture text along with explanations for key words and ideas within that text. This section also includes most of the content designed to produce and maintain discussion within the group.

3. LIVE IT OUT.

The final section focuses on application, using bulleted summary statements to answer the question, *So what?* As the leader, be prepared to challenge the group to apply what they learned during the discussion by transforming it into action throughout the week.

For group leaders, the *Awake* Leader Guide contains several features and tools designed to help you lead participants through the material provided.

QUESTION 1—ICEBREAKER

These opening questions and/or activities are designed to help participants transition into the study and begin engaging the primary themes to be discussed. Be sure everyone has a chance to speak, but maintain a low-pressure environment.

DISCUSSION QUESTIONS

Each "What Does the Bible Say?" section features at least five questions designed to spark discussion and interaction within your group. These questions encourage critical thinking, so be sure to allow a period of silence for participants to process the question and form an answer.

The *Awake* Leader Guide also contains follow-up questions and optional activities that may be helpful to your group, if time permits.

DVD CONTENT

Each video features Dr. Ronnie Floyd discussing the primary themes found in the session. We recommend that you show this video in one of three places: (1) At the beginning of group time, (2) After the icebreaker, or (3) After a quick review and/or summary of "What Does the Bible Say?" A video summary is included as well. You may choose to use this summary as background preparation to help you guide the group.

The Leader Guide contains additional questions to help unpack the video and transition into the discussion. For a digital Leader Guide with commentary, see the "Leader Tools" folder on the DVD-ROM in your Leader Kit.

For helps on how to use *Bible Studies for Life*, tips on how to better lead groups, or additional ideas for leading, visit: **www.ministrygrid.com/web/BibleStudiesforLife.**

SESSION 1: RETURN TO GOD

The Point: God's call to return to Him demands a response.

The Passage: Jonah 1:1-3; 3:1-5,10

The Setting: Jonah, a prophet in the Northern Kingdom of Israel, had willingly been used by God to deliver a message of encouragement to his nation (see 2 Kings 14:25). However, when God commanded him to deliver a warning message to Nineveh, the capital city of Israel's oppressor, Assyria, Jonah at first refused. Only later, with reluctance, did Jonah comply with God's instruction.

QUESTION 1: What's a great way to catch your attention?

> *Optional activity:* Encourage group members to identify ringtones in their phones that catch their attention. Ask for volunteers to play the tone they consider most attention grabbing and invite them to explain why. If time permits, vote as a group to identify who has the most attention-grabbing ringtone.

Note: Don't attempt this activity if you have encouraged group members not to bring their phones to the group meeting or if you meet in a space where loud noises would be a distraction for others. Rely on your best judgment.

Video Summary: In this opening video session, Dr. Floyd explains that when God wants to do something corporately, He starts with individuals. We see a perfect illustration of that in the story of Jonah. God wanted to return a city to Himself, and He started in the life of Jonah. And what God did in the heart and life of Jonah served as a catalyst for a great spiritual movement in Nineva.

WATCH THE DVD SEGMENT FOR SESSION 1, THEN USE THE FOLLOWING QUESTIONS AND DISCUSSION POINTS TO TRANSITION INTO THE STUDY.

- What is God doing in your life personally that could impact your sphere of influence?
- What do you think God might want to do through your small group for a greater good?

WHAT DOES THE BIBLE SAY?

ASK FOR A VOLUNTEER TO READ ALOUD JONAH 1:1-3; 3:1-5,10.

Response: What's your initial reaction to these verses?

- What do you like about the text?
- What questions do you have about these verses?

TURN THE GROUP'S ATTENTION TO JONAH 1:1-3.

QUESTION 2: Why is it sometimes tempting to flee from God?

This question is intended to give members an opportunity to examine the reasons it may be more tempting to flee from God's call and run toward a place, person, or desire they think will bring fulfillment.

> *Optional follow-up:* What are some ways God speaks to people today?

MOVE TO JONAH 3:1-5.

QUESTION 3: When have you benefited from a second chance?

This question is designed to give group members an opportunity to share a personal story. Don't force people to answer what could be a deeply personal question. At the same time, don't discourage people from being vulnerable if they choose to do so.

> *Optional follow-up:* When have you been in a position to offer someone else a second chance?

QUESTION 4: What do God's actions toward Jonah and the Ninevites teach us about His character?

Encourage group members to examine the text closely. This question will require them to personally interpret what God's actions in Jonah 3:1-5 teach us about His character.

> *Optional follow-up:* What are the different ways people responded to God in these verses?

CONTINUE WITH JONAH 3:10.

QUESTION 5: How can our group be a safe and supportive place for returning to God?

Ending your group time with an application question should leave group members with a sense of action. Encourage them to be specific in answering as they examine together the ways their group is already safe and supportive as well as how they can make it more so.

> *Optional activity:* Direct group members to complete the activity "Personal Assessment: Wake Up Call" on page 11. Encourage them to complete this activity during the week as a way of exploring their own spiritual health.

Note: The following question does not appear in the group member book. Use it in your group discussion as time allows.

QUESTION 6: Our nation needs to return to God. What must happen in our personal lives for that to occur?

It's common to ask the question, "How can I make a difference? I'm only one person." This question calls for group members to dig deep into their own lives and identify specific changes they can make and ways they can impact a nation that needs to return to God.

LIVE IT OUT

Encourage group members to consider the following ways they can be open to God's call and answer when it comes:

- **Be sensitive to God's voice.** Don't let yourself become numb toward God. Immerse yourself in Bible study and prayer, asking God to help you be more sensitive to His voice.

- **Respond with obedience.** When you hear God telling you to do something in the days to come—do it! Repentance isn't necessary when we obey God's call in the first place.

- **Repent when necessary.** None of us will obey perfectly. When you find yourself wandering from God, repent, turn away from your disobedience, and turn back to God.

Challenge: As we saw in Jonah's story, God often acts to get our attention and draws us back to Himself. Could He be trying to get your attention right now? Spend time in prayer this week asking God to make you aware of areas in your life where He may be trying to draw you back to Himself. Be willing to say yes, even before He asks you to respond.

Pray: Ask for prayer requests and ask group members to pray for the different requests as intercessors. As the leader, conclude your discussion by thanking God for the way He demonstrates His grace through second chances. Thank Him for the second chances you've received in life and ask for the courage to respond well when you hear God's call.

SESSION 2: RETURN TO YOUR FIRST LOVE

The Point: Return to a love for Christ that permeates everything you do.

The Passage: Revelation 2:1-7

The Setting: The apostle John found himself on the island of Patmos, probably as a political prisoner of Rome for preaching the gospel. While there, he received an extensive revelation from God regarding the outcome of the conflict between the forces of God and the forces of evil. The revelation begins with a "state of the churches" address.

QUESTION 1: What hobbies or interests have you lost touch with over the years?

Note: If time permits, encourage group members to share what they originally found appealing about those hobbies or interests.

> *Optional activity:* Bring magazines and/or newspapers to the group meeting. Distribute them to your group members and ask them to tear out pages that connect with one of the following: 1) hobbies or interests they have lost touch with over the years or 2) hobbies or interests they would like to pursue in the future.

Video Summary: This week Dr. Floyd talks about the message that John was charged to pass along to the church at Ephesus—it had lost its first love. It was in a very dangerous position. Every church should be defined by its love for Jesus. A church defined by a powerful love for Jesus starts with individuals whose lives are defined by a powerful love for Jesus.

WATCH THE DVD SEGMENT FOR SESSION 2, THEN USE THE FOLLOWING QUESTIONS AND DISCUSSION POINTS TO TRANSITION INTO THE STUDY.

- How have you experienced a wandering from your first love?
- In what ways do you think your return to Christ can impact your church? Your community?

WHAT DOES THE BIBLE SAY?

ASK FOR A VOLUNTEER TO READ ALOUD REVELATION 2:1-7.

Response: What's your initial reaction to these verses?

- What questions do you have about these verses?
- What do you hope to learn this week about how to return to your passion for Christ?

TURN THE GROUP'S ATTENTION TO REVELATION 2:1-4.

QUESTION 2: How would you compare and contrast doing things for Jesus and spending time with Jesus?

In order to answer this question, group members must be able to identify the difference between doing things for Jesus and spending time with Him. If you have space, consider asking a volunteer to record group members' answers on a white board or large sheet of paper. Keeping a visual record is a great way to organize the group's thoughts.

Optional follow-up: If Jesus looked at our church and said, "I know your works," what do you think He would say next?

QUESTION 3: How can we evaluate whether we've lost our first love for Christ?

To identify whether or not they have lost their passion for Christ, group members need to be able to recognize actions, attitudes, or behaviors that indicate they have drifted. Encourage them to be specific in their responses.

Optional activity: Direct group members to complete the activity "First Love" on page 19. If you have time, encourage volunteers to share how they felt during their earliest experiences with Christ.

MOVE TO REVELATION 2:5-7.

QUESTION 4: What does it look like for a follower of Christ to repent?

Answering this question calls for group members to first answer the question: What does it mean to repent? Once that question has been answered, encourage group members to identify the attitude, behavior, and mindset required for true repentance.

Optional follow-up: How has your relationship with Jesus changed over time?

QUESTION 5: How do we train ourselves to listen to God's Spirit throughout the day?

You may wish to start your discussion of this question by pointing group members back to the list on page 21 and the three things the Spirit had to say to the church at Ephesus as well as to us.

Optional follow-up: What are some costs and benefits of actively listening to God?

Note: The following question does not appear in the group member book. Use it in your group discussion as time allows.

QUESTION 6: When people choose to return to God, what obstacles should they expect to encounter?

To answer this question, group members must first identify common obstacles they encounter when they choose to return to God. Through identifying these obstacles they will then be in a better position to face them when they come.

LIVE IT OUT

Invite group members to consider these suggestions for how they can return to their first love as they follow Christ in the days to come:

- **Remember.** Write down the top three things that describe your Christian walk at its most healthy.
- **Repent.** Spend time identifying any habits or patterns in your life that are detrimental to your love for Jesus. Repent before God right now. Turn from those sins today.
- **Return.** Write down a practical plan for drawing closer to God. This may be a renewed commitment to daily Bible reading, prayer, sharing your faith, and so on.

Challenge: The wonderful thing about the grace of Jesus is that it doesn't matter where we've been or what we've done—His grace is greater. Take some time this week to write down specific actions you are taking to draw closer to Jesus again as well as ways you see Him bringing back your love for Him.

Pray: Ask for prayer requests and ask group members to pray for the different requests as intercessors. As the leader, conclude the discussion by affirming that Jesus deserves the primary place in your life, and in the lives of your group members. Ask God to bless all of you with a renewed passion for Christ.

SESSION 3: RETURN TO PRAYER

The Point: Move forward by retreating into prayer.

The Passage: Nehemiah 1:3-10

The Setting: Nearly a century and a half had lapsed since the southern kingdom of Judah had fallen to Babylon and God's people ceased to be an independent nation. During that time, the Medes and Persians had taken control of Babylon and all its territory. Cyrus, the new king, permitted the captive to return to Jerusalem, and a new temple was constructed in Jerusalem. Yet Nehemiah, cupbearer to the Persian king, learned the city itself remained unprotected.

QUESTION 1: How do you typically respond to bad news?

Optional activity: This session is focused on the discipline of prayer, which is something that can become stale in a group setting—especially when a group prays in the same way week in and week out. Therefore, shake things up a bit by asking group members to find a new position or posture in which to pray. This can include kneeling, standing, walking, joining hands, and so on. As you join together in prayer, use this time to ask the Lord to prepare your hearts for what He has for you in your study this week.

Note: Be sure to take your meeting space into account when deciding whether to use this activity. Also consider the needs of any group members who may have difficulty moving around.

Video Summary: This week's video message is about the power of prayer as illustrated through the life of Nehemiah. Nehemiah received word that the people of Israel were in trouble, the wall around Jerusalem had been broken down and its gates destroyed. Instead of going to work to fix the problem or ordering the people to get to work rebuilding the wall, Nehemiah first turned to God in prayer and fasting. He allowed desperation in his own life to drive him to desperation for God.

WATCH THE DVD SEGMENT FOR SESSION 3, THEN USE THE FOLLOWING QUESTIONS AND DISCUSSION POINTS TO TRANSITION INTO THE STUDY.

- Where do you run when you are desperate?
- Dr. Floyd says, "No great movement of God has ever taken place that wasn't preceded by extraordinary prayer." What difference can you make by choosing to turn to God first in prayer?

WHAT DOES THE BIBLE SAY?

ASK FOR A VOLUNTEER TO READ ALOUD NEHEMIAH 1:3-10.

Response: What's your initial reaction to these verses?

- What questions do you have about these verses?
- What new application do you hope to get from this passage?

TURN THE GROUP'S ATTENTION TO NEHEMIAH 1:3.

QUESTION 2: What are some symptoms of spiritual trouble in today's culture?

You can use the third paragraph on page 28 as a way of transitioning into this discussion question. Jerusalem's broken walls reflected the spiritual desperation of its people. In the same way, what elements of modern culture reveal our need for God?

Optional follow-up: What are some symptoms of spiritual trouble in today's church?

MOVE TO NEHEMIAH 1:4-6a.

QUESTION 3: Nehemiah responded with mourning, praying, and fasting. When should we incorporate these practices in our lives?

This question allows group members an opportunity to process, through the filter of the biblical text, why and when mourning, praying, and fasting are important.

Optional activity: Direct group members to complete the activity "Location, Location, Location" on page 29. If time permits, encourage volunteers to share their favorite locations for prayer.

CONTINUE WITH NEHEMIAH 1:6b-10.

QUESTION 4: What role should confession play in our lives?

Much like Question 3, this question gives group members an opportunity to examine, through the context of Nehemiah 1:6b-10, the reason for and importance of confession in our lives.

> ***Optional follow-up:*** In what practical ways can you position yourself to be a more active part of bringing about revival in your circles of influence?

QUESTION 5: What's one step you could take to improve your prayer life?

This question requires group members to identify and share a specific action they can take to improve their prayer lives. It promotes accountability and the need to act on biblical truth.

> ***Optional follow-up:*** What's one step we could take to improve our group's prayer life?

Note: The following question does not appear in the group member book. Use it in your group discussion as time allows.

QUESTION 6: What are some appropriate goals and desires for our experiences with prayer?

Answering this question will require group members to define for themselves the purpose and importance of prayer and the role they wish for it to play in their lives.

LIVE IT OUT

Encourage group members to consider the following suggestions for how they can move forward with God this week:

- **Pray every day.** Stop trying to fix your problems on your own and take your problems to the only One who can really solve them.

- **Schedule time for uninterrupted prayer.** Block out at least 15-30 minutes for longer experiences with prayer. Guard that time and use it to focus on God as you pray for revival for yourself, your family, your church, and your community.

- **Fast.** Fasting can take your prayer life to a new level. Consider fasting as a group on a particular day.

Challenge: In today's Scripture we witnessed how Nehemiah was faced with a mountain of bad news. He responded by turning to God in prayer. And Nehemiah's example can help us do the same. This week when the struggles come, make prayer your first course of action.

Pray: Ask for prayer requests and ask group members to pray for the different requests as intercessors. As the leader, conclude the discussion by again thanking God for the privilege of prayer. Ask that His Spirit would convict each person in your group regarding specific disciplines and practices that would enhance their focus on prayer.

The Point: God's Word is the fuel for a consistent lifestyle.

The Passage: Nehemiah 8:1-8

The Setting: The work of rebuilding the fortified wall around Jerusalem went surprisingly quick—52 days to be exact (see Neh. 6:15). But Nehemiah's work in Jerusalem did not end with the completion of the wall. For at least 12 years he served as governor of Judah (see 5:14). At some point following the restoration of the wall and while Nehemiah was governor, he and Ezra the scribe led the people in a renewal of their covenant with God.

QUESTION 1: When has following someone's directions taken you someplace unexpected?

This is a great opportunity to encourage group members to share specific stories. Don't feel bad about asking for more information after an initial answer.

> *Optional activity:* Encourage group members to share their best shortcuts and driving tips for different locations in your area. You can ask for general driving tips in your community or shortcuts to specific locations—how to get downtown the fastest, the best route to the nearest airport, how to avoid paying tolls, which specific roads or intersections to avoid, etc.

Note: If your group members have smart phones with GPS applications, you could encourage everyone to use their phones when identifying specific locations.

Video Summary: This week's study transitions from the picture of brokenness and devastation in Nehemiah 1 to the picture of celebration in Nehemiah 8. As Ezra stood and read from the Word of God for up to six hours a day, the attentiveness of the crowd represented God's movement among the people. He was bringing revival to His church as represented through their increased desire for His Word. They were gripped by God and couldn't help but respond to what they were hearing.

WATCH THE DVD SEGMENT FOR SESSION 4, THEN USE THE FOLLOWING QUESTIONS AND DISCUSSION POINTS TO TRANSITION INTO THE STUDY.

- On a scale of 1 to 10, how responsive are you to the Word of God? Explain.
- In what ways are you building your life on the Word of God?

WHAT DOES THE BIBLE SAY?

ASK FOR A VOLUNTEER TO READ ALOUD NEHEMIAH 8:1-8.

Response: What's your initial reaction to these verses?

- What do you like about the text?
- What new application do you hope to receive about the important role the Bible plays in a sustained, close walk with God?

TURN THE GROUP'S ATTENTION TO NEHEMIAH 8:1-3.

QUESTION 2: How do our circumstances impact the way we approach the Bible?

This question will give group members an opportunity to examine how their own personal experiences color their relationship with the Bible.

> **Optional activity:** Direct group members to complete the activity "Fuel Stop" on page 39. If time permits, encourage volunteers to share their responses.

MOVE TO NEHEMIAH 8:4-6.

QUESTION 3: What's the connection between engaging the Bible and worshiping God?

You may want to begin your discussion of this question by more closely examining Ezra's actions in this passage. After talking about what Ezra was doing, move the group to talk more specifically about what his actions can teach us about the connection between engaging the Bible and worshiping God.

> **Optional follow-up:** What prevents us from responding more meaningfully and more consistently to God's Word?

CONTINUE WITH NEHEMIAH 8:7-8.

QUESTION 4: When have you recently been affected or convicted by your study of God's Word?

This question asks group members to recall a personal experience. It may be difficult for some to answer. Therefore, allow group members time to process through their emotions and decide what they feel comfortable sharing. The objective is for each member to understand ways in which he or she has been impacted by the study of God's Word.

> **Optional follow-up:** How has your relationship with the Bible changed over time?

QUESTION 5: What steps can you take to better understand and apply God's Word?

Encourage group members to do some self-examination before they respond. As time allows, also invite them to share action steps for strengthening the way they interact with God's Word.

> **Optional follow-up:** What steps can our group take to better understand and apply God's Word?

Note: The following question does not appear in the group member book. Use it in your group discussion as time allows.

QUESTION 6: What questions would you like to have answered about the role of the Bible in their daily lives?

Hopefully group members will feel comfortable enough in your group to ask questions they may have. Be willing to start this discussion yourself to help others feel more comfortable It's likely that both believers and non-believers have or have had questions regarding the role of the Bible in our daily lives.

LIVE IT OUT

Encourage group members to consider the following ideas for making sure the Scriptures have their rightful place in their lives.

- **Read up.** Make a habit of reading the Bible every day. A devotional book or magazine can help you get started, but give God uninterrupted time to speak through His Word.

- **Listen up.** Make yourself more attentive to God's Word by taking notes. Write down what you hear God saying to you.

- **Step up.** Lead a small group or Bible study. Teach children or students at your church. The greatest way to learn the Scriptures is to teach them to someone else!

Challenge: God gave us a roadmap for life—one that never fails. This map, His Word, gives us His directions on how to live and is our fuel for spiritual renewal. If you don't currently have a Bible reading plan in place, consider starting one. If you aren't sure where to begin, search online for an option that best fits you.

Pray: Ask for prayer requests and ask group members to pray for the different request as intercessors. As the leader, conclude the discussion by praising God for the value of His Word in your life and in the lives of your group members. Commit to reading and applying the Scriptures each day as you seek to serve God.

SESSION 5: RETURN TO UNITY

The Point: Walking with Christ brings us together in unity and purpose.

The Passage: Acts 4:31-37

The Setting: Pentecost saw the Holy Spirit descend on Jesus' followers, Peter boldly proclaim the gospel to an international crowd, and 3,000 people come to faith. A short time later, Peter and John encountered a lame man in the temple courtyard, whom they healed. That event, coupled with the disciples' preaching, resulted in the arrest of Peter and John. Upon their release, the two gathered with other believers and prayed for boldness to proclaim the gospel.

QUESTION 1: When have you felt united with others in a common cause?

Remind group members that their answers do not have to be "spiritual."

Optional activity: Use the following activity to add some physical movement to your group experience and reinforce the theme of finding unity in Christ. Encourage group members to gather in smaller groups based on their answers to the questions below. Have them answer the questions one at a time and regroup with each.

- What is your favorite sport?

- What is your favorite color?

- In your opinion, what's the best restaurant within five miles of your group?

- In what state were you born?

Video Summary: In this week's message, Dr. Floyd talks about the importance of unity in the church. Acts 4 is a powerful picture of the church coming together in unity. The church was being persecuted for spreading the gospel. But despite the fact that they could have been punished for their actions, the early believers chose to pray to God for boldness to keep preaching. Few things bring people together like a crisis. And these believers truly lived as one body rather than individual members of one body.

WATCH THE DVD SEGMENT FOR SESSION 5, THEN USE THE FOLLOWING QUESTIONS AND DISCUSSION POINTS TO TRANSITION INTO THE STUDY.

- Is there currently conflict that you are a part of? Explain.
- What do you need to do to settle the conflict and move toward unity?

WHAT DOES THE BIBLE SAY?

ASK FOR A VOLUNTEER TO READ ALOUD ACTS 4:31-37.

Response: What's your initial reaction to these verses?

- What questions do you have about these verses?
- What new application do you hope to get from this passage?

TURN THE GROUP'S ATTENTION TO ACTS 4:31.

QUESTION 2: What factors help people feel united?

This question requires that group members interpret Acts 4:31 for themselves as a way to move them toward defining what unity is and what factors unite people.

Optional follow-up: When have you seen someone demonstrate boldness for Christ?

Optional activity: Direct group members to complete the activity "Unity and Diversity" on page 49. If time allows, encourage volunteers to share their responses.

MOVE TO ACTS 4:32-33.

QUESTION 3: How have you seen mutual generosity impact your church or community?

It's possible that group members will wander into a discussion about socialism or utopian societies, given that the members of the early church were so free with their possessions. Do your best to keep the group focused by encouraging members to share a story from their own lives or the life of someone they know.

Optional follow-up: How would you describe the purpose of the church?

CONTINUE WITH ACTS 4:34-37.

QUESTION 4: What's your initial reaction to these verses?

This question is designed to encourage group members to actively engage and interpret for themselves the meaning of the Scripture text in order to share their reaction to the verses.

Optional follow-up: What can we surrender to contribute to the unity and purpose of the church?

QUESTION 5: How should these verses guide our actions and attitudes today?

Consider dividing your discussion of this question into two sections: 1) How should these verses guide our actions as individuals; and 2) How should these verses guide our actions as a group?

Note: The following question does not appear in the group member book. Use it in your group discussion as time allows.

QUESTION 6: What are the blessings and benefits of growing in unity as a congregation?

Rather than offering up individual thoughts, encourage group members to work together to answer this question and to be specific in their responses.

Optional follow-up: In what ways have you experienced these blessings and benefits in your own life?

LIVE IT OUT

There is incredible power when God unites His people. Invite group members to consider the following options for how they can strive for unity of heart and mind within their church community:

- **Yield.** Surrender each morning to the lordship of Christ and let Him fill you with His Holy Spirit.
- **Pray.** Pray daily for unity in your church and among believers in your community. Ask God to remove all barriers to unity and make your church family one in heart and mind.
- **Share.** Take a bold step to confirm that you've surrendered everything to Christ. When you see someone with a need this week, do whatever you can do to take care of it.

Challenge: God uses our unity in Him to bring revival to our lives and churches— and that leads to spiritual awakening in our nation. Consider specific, deliberate actions you can take this week to help strengthen unity within your family, your church, and your community.

Pray: Ask for prayer requests and ask group members to pray for the different request as intercessors. As the leader, conclude the discussion by asking the Holy Spirit to move in a powerful way throughout your community and especially within your local church. Ask Him to bless your congregation and the members of your group with a desire to strive for unity as followers of Christ.

SESSION 6: RETURN TO THE TASK

The Point: A revitalized church spreads the gospel.

The Passage: Acts 13:1-3,44-52

The Setting: The spread of the gospel at Pentecost continued its outward push, eventually sweeping over the Gentiles in Antioch. Through the leading of the Holy Spirit, the church sent out Barnabas and Saul on the first missionary journey to spread the gospel even further. As they took the good news to new places, the duo repeatedly met with rejection, repeatedly returned to the task at hand, and repeatedly found receptive hearers.

QUESTION 1: Where do you like to go to recharge your batteries?

Optional activity: Prior to the group meeting, purchase a set of postcards featuring beach scenes from an idyllic location—Hawaii, Fiji, or someplace similar. Write the following three phrases on the back of each card: "Pray. Fast. Share the gospel." Distribute these cards at the beginning of the group meeting as a way of connecting Question #1 with the primary theme of this session or at the end of the group meeting to reinforce your discussion. In either case, encourage group members to place the cards on their refrigerators or in their Bibles as a reminder to seek God and share the good news of His gospel.

Note: You could also consider writing a personal note of encouragement to each of your group members on the backs of the cards. If you do so, be sure to create a couple of extra cards in case you have visitors.

Video Summary: This week's video message focuses on the example set by the church at Antioch. This was a church with a heart to reach people who were different from them. They reached beyond the Jews to the Gentiles and found there a receptive and accepting crowd. They lived out the heartbeat of God in the world. And when we grasp the heart of God as the church at Antioch did, we will be passionate about spreading the gospel, too.

WATCH THE DVD SEGMENT FOR SESSION 6, THEN USE THE FOLLOWING QUESTIONS AND DISCUSSION POINTS TO TRANSITION INTO THE STUDY.

- How have you experienced the connection between grasping the heart of God and being passionate about spreading the gospel?
- In what ways might you be able to strengthen that connection?

WHAT DOES THE BIBLE SAY?

ASK FOR A VOLUNTEER TO READ ALOUD ACTS 13:1-3,44-52.

Response: What's your initial reaction to these verses?

- What questions do you have about how you can be a part of fulfilling the Great Commission?
- What new application do you hope to get from this passage?

TURN THE GROUP'S ATTENTION TO ACTS 13:1-3.

QUESTION 2: What can we do to intentionally seek God's guidance?

This is another question that can be approached in two ways:
1) What can we do as individuals; and 2) What can we do as a group?

Optional follow-up: When is it necessary and/or appropriate to fast as a body of believers?

MOVE TO ACTS 13:44-47.

QUESTION 3: What do these verses teach about the process of sharing the gospel?

The intent of this question is to prompt interaction with the biblical text to help group members answer the question based on the experiences of Paul and Barnabas.

Optional follow-up: What opposition do churches sometimes face when they set out to obey God?

CONTINUE WITH ACTS 13:48-52.

QUESTION 4: How have you experienced resistance in your attempts to make disciples?

This question provides group members an opportunity to share specific instances when they have experienced resistance in their attempts to share the gospel. As they share their responses, encourage members to also share ways they attempted to counteract the resistance. As time allows, invite other group members to share ideas as well.

Optional activity: Direct group members to complete the activity "The Spark of Persecution" on page 61. If time allows, encourage volunteers to share their responses.

QUESTION 5: What steps can we take to strive for revival in our church and community?

This question is designed to help group members leave your session with a plan of action. Encourage them to focus on the difference they can make in the lives of others by allowing God to use them to share His good news.

Optional follow-up: How do you hope to see God move in your life and community?

Note: The following question does not appear in the group member book. Use it in your group discussion as time allows.

QUESTION 6: How do you understand your role in God's call for the church to spread the gospel?

Understanding what Scripture says and applying that message to our own lives are two very different things. This question will give group members an opportunity to verbalize their understanding of the part they are called to play in spreading the gospel. Encourage them to listen closely as other group members share. We can learn much from each other.

LIVE IT OUT

Encourage group members to consider the following suggestions for how they can obey God's call to fulfill the Great Commission:

- **Pray for the lost every day.** Pray specifically for someone who needs the message of Christ. Pray for the gospel to advance in your community and around the world.

- **Share the gospel.** Spreading the gospel isn't just for pastors and preachers. Actively seek out opportunities to share the good news of Christ.

- **Lead your group on mission.** Make plans as a group to proclaim the gospel in a tangible, practical way within your community. Start with prayer and move out from there.

Challenge: In Acts 13 we see how the church at Antioch prayed and fasted. And God did something incredible in their midst. Consider spending some focused time this week seeking Him through prayer and fasting. Ask Him to use this time to revitalize you and lead you to fix your attention on the parts of life that are truly important.

Pray: As the leader, close this final session of *Awake* in prayer. Ask God to clearly convict any person in the group who needs to experience a spiritual awakening. Ask for the Holy Spirit to be present in your group as you move forward in your efforts to serve God and obey His commands.

Note: If you haven't discussed it earlier, decide as a group whether or not you plan to continue to meet together and, if so, what Bible study options you would like to pursue. Visit *LifeWay.com/smallgroups* for help, or if you would like more studies like this one, visit *biblestudiesforlife.com/smallgroups*.

WHERE THE BIBLE MEETS LIFE

Bible Studies for Life® will help you know Christ, live in community, and impact the world around you. If you enjoyed this study, be sure and check out these other available titles.* Six sessions each except where noted.

Pressure Points *by Chip Henderson*

When Relationships Collide *by Ron Edmondson*

Do Over: Experience New Life in Christ *by Ben Mandrell*

Honest to God: Real Questions People Ask *by Robert Jeffress*

Let Hope In *by Pete Wilson*

Productive: Finding Joy in What We Do *by Ronnie and Nick Floyd*

Connected: My Life in the Church *by Thom S. Rainer*

Resilient Faith: Standing Strong in the Midst of Suffering *by Mary Jo Sharp*

Beyond Belief: Exploring the Character of God *by Freddy Cardoza*

Overcome: Living Beyond Your Circumstances *by Alex Himaya*

Storm Shelter: God's Embrace in the Psalms *by Philip Nation*

Ready: Ministering to Those in Crisis *by Chip Ingram*

Like No Other: The Life of Christ *by Tony Evans (8 sessions)*

Like Glue: Making Relationships Stick *by Ben Mandrell*

If your group meets regularly, you might consider Bible Studies for Life as an ongoing series. Available for your entire church—kids, students, and adults—it's a format that will be a more affordable option over time. And you can jump in anytime. For more information, visit **biblestudiesforlife.com**.

biblestudiesforlife.com/smallgroups
800.458.2772 | LifeWay Christian Stores

Additional titles will continue to be released every three months.
Visit website for more information.